ROSALIND HALL

EGYPTIAN TEXTILES

SHIRE EGYPTOLOGY

Cover illustration
The deceased and his family receive libations
from a son, Bunakhtef, in the tomb of Sennudjem (Theban
Tomb 1) at Deir el-Medina, Nineteenth Dynasty.
(Photograph by Rosalind Hall.)

British Library Cataloguing in Publication Data available.

Published by
SHIRE PUBLICATIONS LTD
Cromwell House, Church Street, Princes Risborough,
Aylesbury, Bucks HP17 9AJ, UK

Series Editor: Barbara Adams

ISBN 0 85263 800 0

First published 1986

Set in 11 point Times and printed in Great Britain by
C. I. Thomas & Sons (Haverfordwest) Ltd,
Press Buildings, Merlins Bridge, Haverfordwest, Dyfed.

Contents

4

List of illustrations

Chronology

From Murnane, W. J. *The Penguin Guide to Ancient Egypt*, 1983, and including names of those rulers mentioned in the text.

Neolithic	before 5000 BC	Fayum A
Predynastic	before 3150 BC	
	3150 - 3050	Late Predynastic - Protodynastic
Early Dynastic	3050 - 2613 BC	
	3050 - 2890	Dynasty I
		Horus Djet
	2890 - 2686	Dynasty II
	2686 - 2613	Dynasty III
Old Kingdom	2613 - 2181 BC	
	2613 - 2498	Dynasty IV
	2613 - 2589	Snefru
	2498 - 2345	Dynasty V
	2345 - 2181	Dynasty VI
First Intermediate Period	2181 - 2040 BC	
	2181 - 2040	Dynasties VII-X
	2134 - 2060	Dynasty XI (Theban)
Middle Kingdom	2040 - 1782 BC	
	2060 - 1991	Dynasty XI
	2060 - 2010	Mentuhotep I
	2010 - 1998	Mentuhotep II
	1991 - 1782	Dynasty XII
Second Intermediate Period	1782 - 1570 BC	
	1782 - 1650	Dynasties XIII and XIV (Egyptian)
	1663 - 1555	Dynasties XV and XVI (Hyksos)
	1663 - 1570	Dynasty XVII (Theban)
New Kingdom	1570 - 1070 BC	
	1570 - 1293	Dynasty XVIII
	1504 - 1450	Tuthmosis III
	1498 - 1483	Hatshepsut (?)
	1453 - 1419	Amenophis II
	1419 - 1386	Tuthmosis IV
	1350 - 1334	Amenophis IV/Akhenaten
	1334 - 1325	Tutankhamun
	1293 - 1185	Dynasty XIX
	1279 - 1212	Ramesses II
	1185 - 1070	Dynasty XX
	1182 - 1151	Ramesses III
Third Intermediate Period	1070 - 713 BC	
	1070 - 945	Dynasty XXI
	945 - 712	Dynasty XXII
	828 - 712	Dynasty XXIII
	724 - 713	Dynasty XXIV

Late Period	713 - 332 BC		
		713 - 656	Dynasty XXV (Nubian)
		664 - 525	Dynasty XXVI
		525 - 404	Dynasty XXVII (Persian)
		404 - 399	Dynasty XXVIII
		399 - 380	Dynasty XXIX
		380 - 343	Dynasty XXX (Egyptian/Persian)
Graeco-Roman	332 BC to AD 395		
		332 - 30	Ptolemies
		30 BC - AD 395	Roman Emperors
		284 - 305	Diocletian (The Coptic calendar dates its year number from the accession of Diocletian)
Byzantine Period	AD 323 - 642		
		527 - 565	Justinian I
Islamic Period	AD 642 - 1517		

1
The archaeological importance of textiles

Cloth in the Near East has always played a basic role in housing, animal equipment, clothing and soft furnishings. The vast majority of surviving textiles from Egypt, dating back to as early as the Neolithic Period, derive from tombs. But everyday dress can be found in a funerary context, used both to clothe the deceased and to provide him or her with an accompanying wardrobe in the afterlife. A New Kingdom funeral lament expresses this succinctly with the words 'She who was rich in fine linen, who loved clothes, lies in the cast-off garment of yesterday'. Indeed, as worn-out, frequently repaired domestic fabrics, such as old sheets, towels and clothing, were handed over by relatives to the embalmers for recycling into mummy bandages for the deceased, even funerary linens can provide much domestic information.

Whilst fabrics have survived in much more limited numbers from the houses and rubbish tips of domestic settlement sites, they, together with their companion funerary textiles, have frequently become the neglected cast-off rags of today. Mainly excavated in the nineteenth century, or at the very beginning of the twentieth, often by excavators who failed to utilise or even realise their potential, such textiles have too often lain undiscovered and unconserved in museum basements. Fortunately the situation is now rapidly changing. Modern scientific techniques of conservation and analysis, together with developments in absolute dating methods, have both encouraged the survival and enhanced our knowledge of these often delicate organic remains. Indeed, modern excavations, especially those at settlement sites, such as Tell el-Amarna in Middle Egypt, Quseir al-Qadim on the Red Sea and Qasr Ibrim in Nubia, often include a textile expert as an active member of the expedition team. So the future appears much brighter for a realisation of the value of textile evidence, in both the museum and the field, in building up a composite picture of daily life in antiquity.

The rare and often 'rediscovered' extant garments are of prime importance in that they portray an image of daily dress which is often at total variance with that presented by the tomb reliefs and statuary. The main problem is that these representations are unreliable as they are both idealised and conservative in nature and also tend to depict royalty and the elite class, which comprised only a small percentage of Egyptian society. Art and sculpture, mediums predominantly of a religious character, display the Egyptians in their best clothes for eternity and did not aim to show daily dress. People were often portrayed as in the styles of earlier times, thus harking back to long outmoded fashions. Even representations of working people at their daily tasks are misleading as they can give only an idea of dress worn at certain times of the day.

Only by viewing extant textiles, related artefacts and textual evidence is it possible to ascertain the true picture of daily dress in ancient Egypt and the relevance of the textile industry in Egyptian society.

2
Woven fabrics and dyeing

The predominant woven fabric used in Dynastic Egypt was linen, although coir-type fibres were occasionally used. Wool for clothing appears more frequently than is commonly supposed. Cotton, silk and mohair were all later introductions.

Flax (*Linum usitatissimum*) was used for linen fabrics from as early as the Egyptian Neolithic Period, as evidenced by a fragment from the Fayum A culture of about 5000 BC. The cultivation and preparation of flax can be seen in a number of tomb scenes. It was harvested at different times according to the use to which it was to be put: the young green stems had fibres soft enough for very fine thread; when yellow, the stronger fibres were suitable for good linen cloth; and the tough fibres of the ripe flax could be made into ropes and mats. Once pulled, the flax was rippled by drawing it through a comb-like tool and then retted or soaked to separate the woody parts from the bast fibres. These fibres were further beaten and scraped to remove any remaining bits of stem and were then combed out, after which they were ready to be roved and spun.

Ancient Egyptian linen ranges in colour from white through light brown to golden brown. These colour variations are caused by differences in the maturity of the flax plants and how they were prepared. Some linens were deliberately bleached white. The fabric texture also varies considerably from the finest gauze, with as many as two hundred threads to the inch, to a canvas-like coarse linen. There are basically four qualities of cloth, the Egyptian terms for which, in order of descent, can be translated as 'royal linen', 'fine thin cloth', 'thin cloth', and 'smooth (or ordinary) cloth'. By the Ptolemaic Period there was a considerable cultivation of flax for commercial purposes, with the fine royal or *byssos* linen as the state monopoly of the king himself. Its manufacture was a temple industry, but a fixed quantity had to be delivered to the king for export. However, the smooth cloth was always the most common type available as, in addition to commanding the lowest price, it would have provided better protection against the evening cold when used for garments.

Coir-type fibres such as grass, reed and hemp were also used for woven fabrics other than matting from the Predynastic Period and continuously into Roman times. However, such fabrics are far from common or typical.

The Greek historian Herodotus is responsible for some of our misconceptions regarding the use of wool in ancient Egypt. Writing in the fifth century BC, he relates that it was ceremonially unclean to the Egyptians and that 'nothing of wool is taken into their temples or buried with them for their religion forbids it'. It is now evident that there is much more wool, in both funerary and domestic contexts, than was previously realised, and that it was probably always used for much needed warm clothing, especially cloaks. Herodotus himself mentions the wearing of loose white woollen mantles over linen tunics, whilst the first-century BC Greek author Diodorus Siculus states that the Egyptian sheep yielded 'wool for clothing and ornament'. Certainly the Egyptians would have used the available wool and hair from their large numbers of domesticated sheep and goats. Wool has been found from the Predynastic Period onwards, and a study of wool fibre diameters suggests that it came from a semi-bred sheep of a hairy medium-fleece type. It was dyed and spun in the workmen's villages at Kahun and Amarna. The latter excavations also yielded goat-hair textiles spun from long coarse, dark brown fibre. However, as a selective goat-breeding policy was unknown in Egypt, it has proved impossible to identify the goat type.

Cotton spread westwards from India and the earliest known examples in Egypt bear a possible early third-century BC date. However, most are Roman or later. Although the silkworm was introduced into Europe from China during the reign of Justinian (AD 527-65), isolated earlier silks, but not of the mulberry type, have been found from Ptolemaic Egypt. Mohair, the product of the angora goat, found chiefly in the ancient Levant, is not known in Egypt until the seventh century AD.

The art of dyeing, using natural colours of local origin, was known in Egypt as early as the Predynastic Period, with the textile fibres being invariably spun and then dyed. Analysis of the colours has enabled the dye sources to be identified. The blue dye, the most permanent of the surviving colours, is indigotin, probably woad (*Isatis tinctoria*). Most samples of red dyes are to be identified as madder (*Rubia tinctorium*), but some have proved to be inorganic, perhaps from a red ochreous earth. Henna mixed with a red colour, obtained from the flowers of the plant *Carthamus tinctorius*, which could also yield a yellow dye, is known. Yellow dyes derive from both the safflower and iron buff. Green was formed by double dyeing with both indigotin and a

1. The earliest known Egyptian flax. Neolithic linen fragment from the Fayum A culture, about 5000 BC. (UC 2943.)

yellow dye. A purple thread on a textile from the workmen's village at Amarna was double dyed using both indigotin and madder. Dyed dark brown fabrics from the tomb of Tuthmosis IV were produced by the same technique. This method was common in the Coptic Period for producing a cheap but effective purple colour.

Dyeing requires two mediums, the colour and the chemical agent, or mordant, to fix the dye to the fabric. The problem of obtaining fast colours seems to have been sufficient to have discouraged the use of patterned fabric in ancient Egypt. The principal mordant available was alum, which was mined in ancient times in the Libyan Desert oases. However, there are no certain instances of its use from ancient Egypt although it has been suggested that alum was employed on Twelfth Dynasty mummy bandages from Rifeh. Textual evidence may indicate its presence, as a mordant with madder, during the New Kingdom. The Graeco-Roman dyeing workshop found by Petrie next to the Athribis temple indicates that dyers were temple employees.

3
Spinning and weaving

Spinning and weaving were practised in ancient Egypt from the Neolithic Period, technical evidence being afforded by depictions, models and the surviving artefacts. The craft flourished on all levels as a state, temple and private concern, engaging men, women and children.

The dried flax fibres were initially prepared by roving, the rolling of fibres on the left thigh to create drawn-out and loosely twisted slivers. The roves were wound on pottery reels into balls and placed in pots or tension buckets of stone, pottery or basketry. These possessed interior rings or lids with holes through which the threads passed smoothly for spinning on a spindle.

Egyptian spindles were spun with the whorl uppermost. The few complete examples are slender sticks tapering at the bottom and weighted towards the top with a whorl, both being of wood. Separate whorls of stone or pottery are also found. The typical Middle Kingdom whorl was flat and cylindrical: that of the New Kingdom was domed. The spindle shaft evolved from a deep spiral groove at the top to receive the thread to the later hook cut close to the stem. The distaff did not come into general use in Egypt until the Roman Period.

Most Egyptian thread is s-spun (anti-clockwise), doubtless because flax naturally rotates in this direction when drying, although z-spun (clockwise) yarn is known. Two or more weak threads were frequently twisted together, in the opposite direction to that in which they were spun, to create a plied yarn (capital S or Z). The Egyptian spinners were skilful enough specifically to produce a Z-plied yarn, from s-spun threads, for sewing purposes.

Middle Kingdom tomb reliefs at Beni Hasan, Deir el-Bersheh and Thebes depict partly naked spinners using three different techniques. The most primitive, the *supported spindle*, represents a logical development from simple hand spinning and was especially popular for wool. Single roves were guided from the pot through the fingers on to the spindle, which was rotated by raising one knee and rolling it on the thigh to twist the fibres. A coarse uneven yarn was produced by the *grasped spindle* method, where the rove was drawn out of the pot, through a spinning-ring or over a forked stick, and attached to a large spindle rotated between the palms of the hands. The most popular procedure,

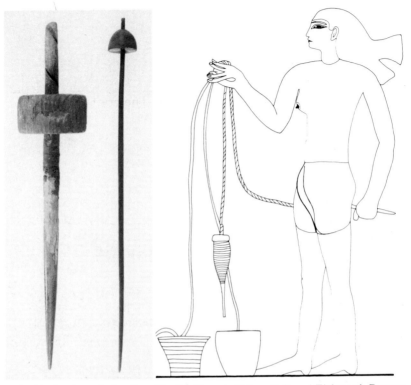

2. (Left) Wooden spindles from Twelfth Dynasty Kahun *(left)* and Eighteenth Dynasty Gurob *(right)* showing the distinct forms. (UC 7306i and UC 7809.)

3. (Right) Girl twining spun threads to create a plied yarn. From the tomb of Khnemhotep at Beni Hasan, Twelfth Dynasty (after Griffith, *Beni Hasan*, IV, 1900, plate XV).

the *suspended spindle*, produced a very fine even thread. The rove was drawn through the left-hand fingers and attached to the spindle, which was rotated and allowed to drop and swing, the weight of the whorl maintaining the spin. Both scenes and models depict the remarkable feat of spinning with two spindles from a single pot, enabling the doubling of four threads simultaneously.

Egyptian looms were of two types, the earliest being the frameless horizontal ground-loom. It is first represented on a Predynastic pottery dish, now in the Petrie Museum at University College London, originating from a woman's grave 3802 at Badari. The interior design, in cream on red, clearly shows a ground-loom with the warp stretched between two beams with four pegs at the corners. Three lines cross the centre, possibly

4. Two groups of rovers and spinners. From the tomb of Khety at Beni Hasan, Twelfth Dynasty. (After Newberry, *Beni Hasan*, II 1893, plate XIII.)

indicating rods keeping the division between odd and even threads. The three lines at the right represent three throws of weft. By the loom lies an unidentified implement, possibly a comb. Above, two men hang strands over a pole. This simple loom was ideal for a nomadic people as the pegs could be pulled out and the weaving rolled up on the beams for transport.

The horizontal ground-loom was used exclusively in Egypt until the end of the Middle Kingdom and is illustrated in various contemporary tomb scenes, such as those of Baqt and Khety at Beni Hasan, and wooden models. If the loom in the tomb of Khnemhotep at Beni Hasan appears to be vertical, this is only because of Egyptian drawing conventions. The splendid model of a weaving workshop found by Winlock in 1920 in the tomb of the Chancellor Meket-Re at Deir el-Bahri (Theban Tomb 280) shows two operational ground-looms and additionally depicts roving, spinning and warping. Remains of pegs at the workmen's village at Amarna indicate that warping, in a figure of eight, was performed both on street walls and inside the houses.

The vertical-framed loom with two beams came into use by the early New Kingdom and probably represents an introduction of the Hyksos Dynasties, which derived from the Near East. Although its introduction encouraged tapestry weaving, it by no means entirely displaced the horizontal ground-loom. The vertical loom is seen in three Eighteenth Dynasty Theban tomb paintings, which, although unfortunately much damaged, can be reconstructed to show the component parts. The warp is stretched between two beams, fastened in a rectangular wooden frame, by the weaver, who sits or squats at the work at the loom base.

Both looms employed the same technique for dividing warp threads. The odd-number threads were lashed to the heddle rod and raised to create a space (shed) through which the weft thread passed. The space (countershed) for the return of the weft, attached to a shuttle, was made by turning on edge the flat shed rod through the weft. A long flat wand, the beater-in, closed up the wefts.

The simplest form of weaving was the plain (tabby) weave, where one weft thread (pick) passed over and under the warp threads (ends). In the next row (throw) the pick passed under one end and over the next, so forming an interlocking structure. All other weaves were simply variations on this theme, although

5. A pottery dish depicting a horizontal ground-loom, from tomb 3802 at Badari, Predynastic. (UC 9547.)

6. Horizontal ground-looms. From the tombs of Baqt, Khety (mat-loom) and Khnemhotep at Beni Hasan, Twelfth Dynasty. (After Newberry, *Beni Hasan*, I, 1893, plate XXIX, and *Beni Hasan*, II, 1893, plates IV and XIII.)

some could be extremely complex. Remarkably few surviving Egyptian textiles bear any weaving faults. Weaves with pile, popular for towels, covers and garments, were formed by inserting extra threads parallel to the weft or warp of a ground weave to create a pattern in tufts or loops. Selvedges and edges frequently display weft and warp fringes, one of the main decorative elements on Pharaonic textiles. These were originally short uncut loops, which, through wear and deterioration, have now become untwisted. Particular fringe construction methods, in addition to identifying weaver's marks set into the selvedge, represent trademarks of individual ateliers.

As a state industry, weaving was particularly the concern of the royal harem. Evidence from the permanent New Kingdom harem established at Gurob (ancient Mi-Wer) in the Fayum indicates that many of its inmates were responsible for cloth manufacture. Although the ladies may have undertaken some of the more delicate work themselves to occupy their time, their prime task was the training, instruction and supervision of the textile workers. Assisted by officials, they were all directly accountable to the overseer of the harem and his deputy, who undertook the administration. The workers, from amongst the local inhabitants, were state-employed in spinning, weaving, sewing and netting, either in workshops or as a home-based industry. A fragmentary papyrus letter refers to their training and also records in detail the harem stores of garments and cloth which were sent either to the king or to various houses. Some linens were specifically intended for the Hittite princess whom Ramesses II married in his thirty-fourth regnal year.

All Egyptian temples seem to have possessed weaving ateliers. Garments manufactured there were bartered, through professional traders using cargo boats, for commodities such as sesame

7. A wooden model of a weaving workshop, from the tomb of Meket-Re at Deir el-Bahri, Eleventh Dynasty. (JE 46723. Courtesy of the Egyptian Museum, Cairo.)

8. The grasped spindle method and vertical looms in operation in the Theban town house of Djehutynefer, Eighteenth Dynasty. (After Davies, in *Metropolitan Museum Studies*, I, 1929, fig. 1 on page 234.)

oil. 'Royal linen' was produced for priestly vestments, clothing the divine statues and royal funerary use. The unidenitified Delta town of Tait was associated with weaving and there Tait, the local goddess, allegedly supervised stores of temple cloth. Funerary garments and wrappings, likewise under Tait's control, were imbued with magical force. The *Annals* of Tuthmosis III report that Syrian captives were 'clothmakers' on the estate of Amun at Karnak, possibly instructing the Egyptians in the Asiatic art of tapestry weaving. The same Pharaoh presented 150 Asiatic weavers to one chief official.

Judging by workshop models and reliefs, private estates employed their own weavers. The Theban town house of Djehutynefer (Theban Tomb 104) shows spinning, weaving and baking being performed on the ground or basement floor, reserved as domestics' quarters and workrooms. As a domestic concern, both sexes frequently engaged in home weaving. At Deir el-Medina the workmen sometimes made weaving and sewing activities an excuse for absence from work. Both crafts were evidently undertaken as part of the village barter system.

In the New Kingdom, the majority of the known overseers of weavers, sometimes women, were employed on the Karnak estates, including the Theban royal mortuary temples, although managers on royal and private estates are also attested. The higher two grades took no part in the actual work, which was directed by petty officials in the lower two classes who managed either whole ateliers or specialised departments. A long list of overseers, perhaps temple personnel, mentions one 'chief of the dressmakers', possibly indicating a professional tailor. However, whether this title is different from a 'chief weaver', who does not occur in the list, is uncertain.

Textile workers on all estates comprised men, women and children. Women, from the Middle Kingdom onwards frequently Asiatics, usually roved and spun, but men and children were also spinners. Men usually beat the flax stems and twined the spun thread. Whilst the weavers on the horizontal ground-loom were invariably women, the mat and vertical looms were operated exclusively by men. The New Kingdom copy of the composition *The Satire on the Trades* contains a passage lamenting the weaver's task: 'The mat-weaver in the workshop, he is worse off than a woman [in childbirth]; with knees against his belly, he cannot breathe air. If he skips a day of weaving, he is beaten with fifty strokes; he gives food to the doorkeeper, to let him see the daylight.'

Whether or not this represents a jaundiced picture is uncertain. Nevertheless it is astonishing that, despite crude equipment, the Egyptian weavers were skilful enough to produce cloth of such remarkably fine texture.

4
Representations of costume

A chronological survey of ancient Egyptian costume based on relief and statuary indicates that, although the basic dress styles, invariably of white linen, were initiated in the Old Kingdom, fashions tended to become progressively more elaborate. Occasion and occupation could also influence design, and women's fashion was uniformly more conservative, displaying less choice of style.

In the Old Kingdom men habitually wore a kilt, fashioned by wrapping a rectangular length of material around the hips. Frequently pleated, this garment was tied tightly around the torso using a variety of methods, either held frontally by its upper corners, by attached ties, or overlapped in front and secured by a girdle. Sometimes its lower end could be extended to form a rigid triangular projection. Certain types of kilt may have been restricted to wearers of particular social classes. Labourers, for instance, generally wore only a sash looped around the waist, leaving long flowing ends in front.

Long garments for both sexes, and similar clothing for the upper torso, displayed fastening ties on one shoulder. The hunter from the mastaba of Ptah-hotep at Saqqara wears such a cloak, displaying rare colourful horizontal stripes in red, blue and yellow, with a green top band. Irregularly grouped small dots further indicate that its fabric was probably dyed or painted skins.

From the Old Kingdom onwards women donned a plain sheath dress stretching from breast to ankles and secured by shoulder straps. Representations showing a form-fitting garment, often with the breasts exposed, simply reflect the artist's desire to reveal the female contours, devoid of underwear, beneath! Women's cloaks sometimes had one or both shoulders starched to a point.

In the Middle Kingdom the kilt continued to be the principal item of male attire, often as a second garment under a longer transparent overskirt. Sometimes pleated, this skirt reached halfway down the calf, invariably hanging lower in front. High-waisted kilts also came into vogue, and occasionally a number were worn simultaneously. In the second half of this period, a long cloak, draped over one or both shoulders, frequently enveloped the body like a blanket. Female dress continued in the Old Kingdom mode.

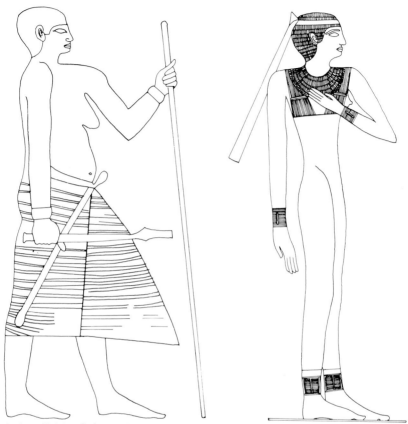

9. An official and his wife at Giza, Sixth Dynasty. (After Simpson, *The Mastabas of Qar and Idu*, 1976, figs. 25 and 34.)

At the beginning of the New Kingdom, earlier fashions were elaborated upon, and clothing for the upper torso was rendered more stylish. Men frequently wore the bag-tunic, a sack-like shirt, in combination with the usual kilt. Occasionally a transparent shawl, draped over the left shoulder and tied at the back, was added. Later in the era mantles covering both shoulders were also worn.

The restrained and simple tastes of earlier ages succumbed to fussiness and frivolity in the later Eighteenth Dynasty, because of the demands of a large empire. A long bag-tunic, plain or pleated, and reaching to the ankles, was the rule. Displaying either long or cap sleeves, it was worn with an apron-like sash,

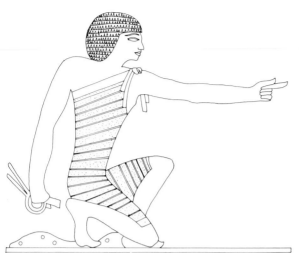

10. A cloaked hunter, Fifth Dynasty. (After Davies, *The Mastabas of Ptahhetep and Akhethetep at Saqqareh*, I, 1900, plate XVIII.)

formed from a second pleated length of fabric, wrapped around the buttocks and tied in front. Its free ends formed a triangular apron, with a fringed selvedge enhancing the decorative effect. By the Ramesside Period this outer apron was loosely tucked up at the bottom to reveal the underskirt.

Women in the early New Kingdom wore sheath dresses, and occasionally bag-tunics. But by the mid Eighteenth Dynasty an increasingly elaborate, voluminous, diaphanous and most commonly pleated dress was depicted. Consisting of a large 'cloak', or wide rectangular cloth, wound around the lower torso, it was draped over the shoulders so that the two weft fringes hung down the front. It was held in place by knotting or a tied sash beneath the breasts. Such a cloak could be worn by priests but was probably not generally used by men.

Priests also wore a short sash across one shoulder, and the ceremonial leopardskin garment became a badge of priestly office. As such it was draped around the body, over the usual clothing, passing under one arm and fastened on the opposite shoulder with head or tail downward. It was depicted either in the form of the single skin or as a simulated painted cloth with spots, polka-dots, five-pointed stars or rosettes.

Royal dress varied considerably according to immediate occupation, but the Pharaoh's corselet, kilt and girdle were traditional garments from the Old Kingdom. By the Ramesside

11. An official and his wife, Eighteenth Dynasty. (After Davies, *The Tomb of Nefer-Hotep at Thebes*, I, 1933, plate XLI.)

Period, the kilt had become more exaggerated in form, and its pendant apron larger, with more elaborate decoration using metal and coloured inlay. The corselet with braces was superseded by the short-sleeved jerkin, or 'king's jacket', often depicted in battle reliefs, complete with its protective falcon device. It had narrow strips which covered the back shoulder blades, were sewn together to form sleeves and tapered into long bands crossed in front of the body, then behind, and finally brought forward to be tied below the breast. Coloured royal headcloths were either tapestry-woven or of sized dyed linen. The horizontally striped streamers floating from royal crowns and wigs were either woven or of solid beadwork. Queens' girdles must have been of similar fabric. The use of patterned textiles, seldom represented before the Late New Kingdom, may have been confined to the royal household throughout the Pharaonic Period.

The apparel of deities remained remarkably static from the Old Kingdom onwards, corresponding with general religious conservatism. Indeed the corselet and kilt, with its frontal pendant ornamentation and rear tail, of the early kings were retained as divine costume. Goddesses wore basic sheath dresses often in red

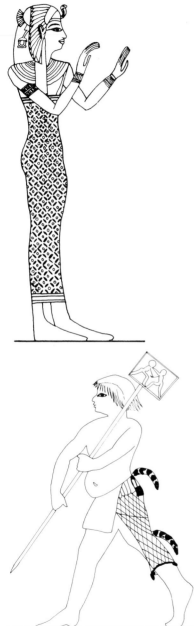

12. (Above) The deified Tuthmosis I and his wife, Queen Ahmose. From the Theban tomb of Userhet, Nineteenth Dynasty. (After Davies, *Two Ramesside Tombs at Thebes*, 1927, plates V and XVI.)

13. (Left) A Nubian mercenary wearing a leather loincloth over a linen one. From the Theban tomb of Tjanuny, Eighteenth Dynasty. (After Davies, *Ancient Egyptian Paintings*, 1936, plate XLV.)

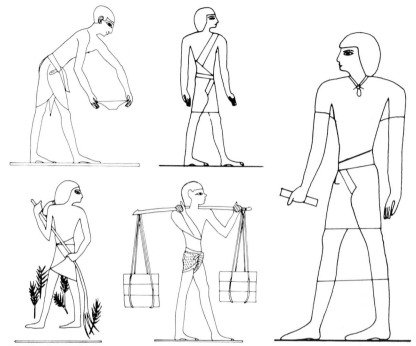

14. The dress of labourers, artisans and an overseer: *(upper left)* kilt with pointed frontal section and belt with long sash ends; *(centre, upper)* kilt and sash; *(lower left)* winnower's kerchief; *(centre, lower)* brickmaker's leather loincloth; *(right)* overseer in long tunic and underskirt. Eighteenth Dynasty. (After Davies, *The Tomb of Rekh-Mi-Re' at Thebes*, 1943, plates LXVII, CVII, LIX, LVI; winnower after Mekhitarian, *La Peinture Égyptienne*, 1954, page 76.)

or blue, cloths of these hues appearing in lists of offerings. Patterned garments using the feather and net motifs were popular because of their magically protective connotations. The former symbolised guardian wings, whilst the latter represented a talisman against evil forces. The fine meshwork garments of goddesses or deified queens simulated bead netting or beaded cloth.

A military-style uniform was worn by Ramesses II's followers, clad in striped leather or wadded linen overgarments, comprising a short cuirass or combined corselet and kilt. Also depicted are coats of mail covered with small metal plates, padded helmets, archers' bracers and quivers of patterned linen. Nubian mercenaries depicted in the tomb of Tjanuny (Theban Tomb 74) wear a leather loincloth over a linen one, with feline tails attached both to the leather itself and to knee garters. This originally Nubian fashion was adopted by Egyptian soldiers, sailors and craftsmen. These pierced leather loincloths displayed either small square holes or a large loose rhomboidal pattern. A kilt of military origin, distinguished by its pointed frontal section and belt with long sash-ends, was in general use by the Eighteenth Dynasty.

Overseers and scribes in charge of workmen were clad in a sometimes transparent long tunic which revealed the underskirt. Labourers' attire comprised only the basic plain kilt, worn either short or below knee length. A loincloth was worn for dirty work by washermen, fishermen, brickmakers and wine pressers. Workers, particularly winnowers, donned a linen kerchief as a dust protector. Labourers' dress could be supplemented with a sash worn over the top of the kilt around the hips, which was sometimes narrow, but in other instances quite wide. Occasionally a long, narrow strip of cloth was bound crosswise around the upper torso, presumably to check perspiration flow. These strips may have been identical to those posing elsewhere as sashes.

Roman and Coptic dress reflected a late classical vogue, deriving little from ancient Egyptian fashions. An interesting intermingling of the Egyptian and Hellenistic styles is seen in the 350 BC tomb of Petosiris, High Priest of Hermopolis, at Tuna el-Gebel.

Unfortunately the representations pose numerous questions. Drawing conventions preclude the exact rendering of tailoring or draping methods. Nor are these garments normal everyday clothing. As an idealised archaism seems to be the pervading rule in funerary art, a faithful rendition of daily dress proves impossible from pictorial evidence, and only the organic remains can provide any solutions.

5
Garments for life and death

Although extant garments are extremely rare, sufficient non-royal dress survives to portray, albeit dimly, both daily and funerary attire. A glimpse of specific types of clothing culminates in an extraordinary entire wardrobe discovered in an architect's unplundered tomb.

In 1977 a dress which might well be the oldest in the world and is certainly the earliest from the Nile valley was discovered in a batch of dirty linen rags belonging to the Petrie Museum. As the linen derived from the large mastaba 2050 at Tarkhan, the garment can be precisely dated to the reign of King Djet, about 2800 BC in the First Dynasty. Although Petrie had not recognised the dress when excavating the mastaba in 1912, he nevertheless fully appreciated the potential of such evidence by retaining the rags.

Splendidly conserved and mounted at The Victoria and Albert Museum, London, this dress consists of a main skirt joined selvedge to selvedge down the left-hand side with an ornamental weft fringe. A stubbed yarn imparts an irregular grey stripe in the warp, deliberately used for decorative effect. No part of the hem remains, but the dress dimensions are those for a young teenager. The sleeves and yoke, cut from two pieces of material, are seamed to the top of the skirt, meeting at centre front and back to form a V-shaped neckline, edged with selvedge. Both sleeves and yoke display tight accordion pleating following the line of shoulder and arm. A right-handed 'tailor' had whipstitched the fabric.

Creasing, particularly round the armpits and elbows, proves that the garment was worn in life. It was also discovered inside out, so, following conservation and application of a silk crêpeline support, the dress was intricately turned right side out. Each pleat having been re-ironed, the elbow crease marks were studied to determine the front and back of the tunic before it was mounted on a frame body shaped to fit.

In 1978 the author discovered two further linen dresses in a jumbled mass of funerary rags at the Petrie Museum. The stronger garment, almost pristine, was wrapped in an 1898 sheet of newsprint from *The Athenaeum* and labelled by Petrie on the outside: 'Galabiyeh. V dyn. Deshasheh.' The weaker dress was found within the linen mass. These garments are two of Petrie's

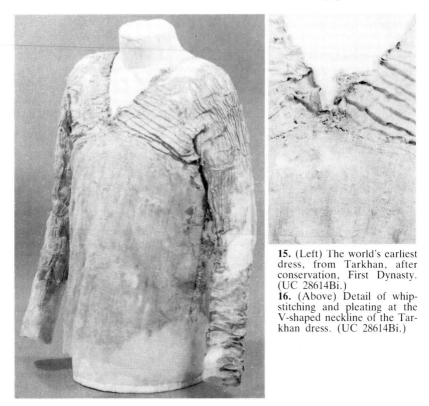

15. (Left) The world's earliest dress, from Tarkhan, after conservation, First Dynasty. (UC 28614Bi.)
16. (Above) Detail of whip-stitching and pleating at the V-shaped neckline of the Tarkhan dress. (UC 28614Bi.)

nine 'shirts' discovered in 1897 in the Fifth Dynasty tomb 148b at Deshasheh, piled directly on top of the female body lying in her wooden coffin. The remaining dresses are now completely lost, but many newly laundered sheets and shawls from the site now reside in the Petrie Museum.

Both garments were subsequently painstakingly conserved and mounted for exhibition, the stronger by the conservator of the Tarkhan dress, and the weaker by a student at the Textile Conservation Centre, Hampton Court Palace. Their pattern style is remarkably similar to the Tarkhan dress, with skirts stretching from waist to feet, likewise displaying extended weft fringes at the left-hand seamed selvedge edges. Rolled hems are visible on the skirt hemline and at the narrow wrists. The V-shaped gaps at front and back were originally closed by three pairs of twisted flax tie-cords. Conservation of the weaker dress revealed interesting 'natural pleating', although it lacked any mechanical pleating. The solid striped weave forced the adjacent loosely woven stripes to turn in an 'S' direction when drying, creating vertical corrugations. Standards of workmanship are generally far cruder than on the Tarkhan dress, as particularly evidenced by clumsy whipstitching.

Both garments are excessively long, at about 55 inches (1400 mm), and extremely narrow, at about 15¾ inches (400 mm). Petrie measured the female body as 53 inches (1350 mm) for the corresponding distance, indicating that the dresses were designed exclusively as grave-goods, a fact substantiated by mummification staining but a total absence of creasing through wear. Spare clothing for the afterlife is an archaic custom, dating back to simple hanks of yarn placed with Predynastic bodies. Pictorial representations in Old Kingdom tomb-chapels at Giza and Saqqara show servants placing long lengths of linen into boxes as funerary equipment, and garments are later depicted on Middle Kingdom coffins. The hieroglyphic determinative for a sleeved garment 𐦤, given in the Old Kingdom linen lists, closely resembles the Tarkhan and Deshasheh dresses.

Two surviving 'fake' burial dresses, sheets cut to simulate the front portions of sheath dresses with V-shaped necklines, were laid directly over female bodies. The earlier plain example, now in the Museum of Fine Arts, Boston, derives from Reisner's 1933 excavations of a Fifth Dynasty Giza burial. A later, horizontally pleated dress with tie-cords was discovered in 1982, by a joint

17. The weaker Deshasheh dress as found in 1979 before conservation. (UC 31183.)

18. (Left) The two lady's dresses from Deshasheh, after conservation, Fifth Dynasty. (UC 31182 and UC 31183.)

19. (Right) An adult female mummy wearing a 'fake' sheath dress from mastaba G2220B at Giza, Fifth Dynasty. (After Reisner, *Giza Necropolis*, I, 1942, plate 42d; now Boston 33.4-22a.)

Hanover/Berlin expedition, in an Eleventh Dynasty tomb at Saqqara.

The closest parallels to the Deshasheh dresses are sleeved garments with overall horizontal pleating excavated at Naga ed-Der, Asyut, Meir and Gebelein, surviving examples residing in the museums of Cairo, Boston, Paris and Turin. The pleating shortened the skirt lengths to about 27½ inches (700 mm), making everyday wear feasible. Indeed, most appear to be made-to-measure garments displaying both creasing and perspiration staining. Doubtless the Deshasheh dresses would have evidenced such pleating had daily use been intended. Where known, these pleated dresses all derive from female burials and indeed represent a logical development from the basic sheath

20. A horizontally pleated dress, one of twelve found on an adult female burial N94, from Naga ed-Der, Sixth Dynasty. (Boston N.94.5. Courtesy of the Museum of Fine Arts, Boston.)

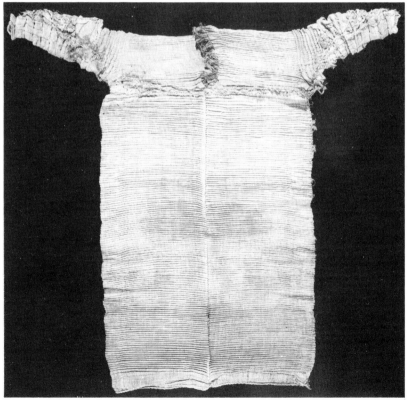

dress. However, the large Asyut dress in the Louvre, found in association with a battleaxe and walking stick, doubtless belonged to a man. Both the provision of sleeves and the extra warmth afforded by the excess pleated fabric suggest that the garments were designed for adverse weather conditions and could well have provided daily protection for agriculturalists. Remarkable similarities to the modern Arab *galabiyeh* indicate that they would have proved equally effective in a hot summer climate. As such they are never represented on the monuments, although a unique sleeveless horizontally pleated tunic appears in one cattle-driving scene. Necessary warm clothing, cloaks, stoles and long kilts, is depicted on Middle Egypt's tomb reliefs, and wool was found in graves at Sedment. These pleated dresses enjoyed only a brief and limited vogue. Doubtless their sagging pleats proved impractical, whilst their clumsy and ugly design was aesthetically unappealing.

It seems that sleeves, which were listed as separate items in laundry lists, could be made separately and attached to garments only when required. The Petrie Museum possesses a fine pair of child's sleeves from New Kingdom Gurob displaying the remains of stitching, indicating that they were once attached to a sleeveless tunic. One of two children's sleeves surviving in the

21. A horizontally pleated cattle driver's tunic *(left)*, from the tomb of Amenemhet at Beni Hasan. A horizontally striped cloak *(right)*, from the tomb of Djehutyhotep at El Bersheh. Twelfth Dynasty. (After Newberry, *Beni Hasan*, I, 1893, plate XIII; and Newberry, *El Bersheh*, I, 1894, plate VII.)

22. A pair of pristine child's sleeves found in tomb 25 at Gurob, Eighteenth to Nineteenth Dynasty. (UC 8980A. and B.)

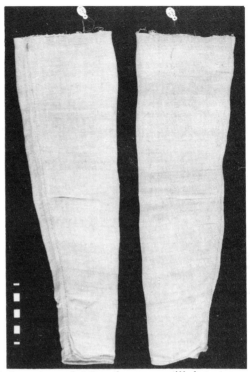

Manchester Museum, University of Manchester, still bears an attached shoulder fragment.

Bag-tunics are reasonably common in museum collections. Examples from the burials of Meket-Re, of Senenmut's mother and of other members of his family show that this type was worn during both the Middle and New Kingdoms. One of the simplest garments, an inverted bag of linen sheeting was formed by a long rectangle folded over and stitched up the sides, a slit being left for the arms, or sleeve attachment if required. A keyhole-shaped cut, placed at or near the fold, sometimes shows a pair of light tie-cords. Varying in length from knee to ankle, their considerable width would have resulted in clumsy folds under the armpits in the absence of gussets. An interesting example in the Petrie Museum displays decorative couching, giving shape to the excess material much in the style of a smock. In Graeco-Roman Egypt the bag-tunic became the principal garment, often bearing applied tapestry-woven motifs in linen and wool.

Irreconcilable divergences are again presented between these

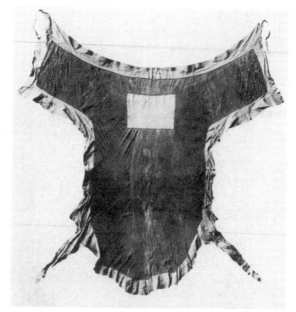

23. Maiherperi's gazelle-skin loincloth, one of two found in his tomb 36 in the Valley of the Kings, Eighteenth Dynasty. (Boston 03.1035. Courtesy of the Museum of Fine Arts, Boston.)

extremely bulky and baggy surviving bag-tunics and the transparent, form-fitting monumental depictions. Extant examples seem to represent the daily working garment of agricultural labourers, rather than being worn solely by overseers and scribes as the depictions would suggest.

Elongated half-cartouche shaped scales, originally applied to leather coats of mail, are attested from the Middle Kingdom tomb of Mesehti at Asyut. Copper/bronze was superseded in the Late Period by iron scale armour.

Eighteenth Dynasty leather loincloths with net patterns display such amazing fineness and fragility that doubts have been cast on their supposed military function. Two examples are on display at the British Museum; two others survive in Boston, their designs corresponding to the two pictorial types. They were discovered by Carter in 1902 lying in a painted box in the tomb of Maiherperi, childhood companion and fan-bearer of Tuthmosis III, honoured with burial in the Valley of the Kings. The illustrated example, with tiny squares precisely cut in the gazelle skin, shows signs of use, with its dextrous ancient mending. The plain leather section was placed over the buttocks, with a linen loincloth under it to protect the skin, and tied around the waist.

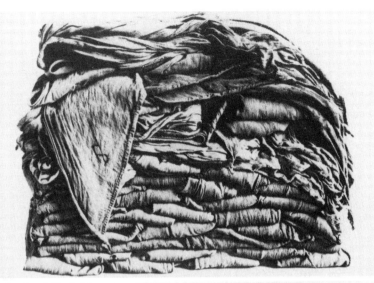

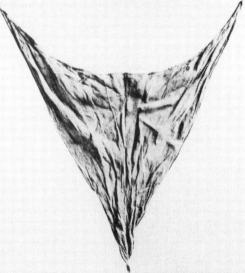

24. A pile of Kha's triangular loincloths *(above)*, with an unfolded example *(right)*. Laundry marks are clearly visible. (After Schiaparelli, *Relazione*, II, 1927, figs. 62 and 64.)

The rounded section was then drawn up between the legs and fastened at the waist in front. Pierced leather garments, mainly women's skirts, are known from Middle Kingdom Nubian sites, principally Kerma and Aniba, and from Second Intermediate pan-graves (burials of Nubian immigrants, mainly mercenaries) in Egypt. Maiherperi himself was at least part Nubian.

The mid Eighteenth Dynasty intact tomb of the architect Kha

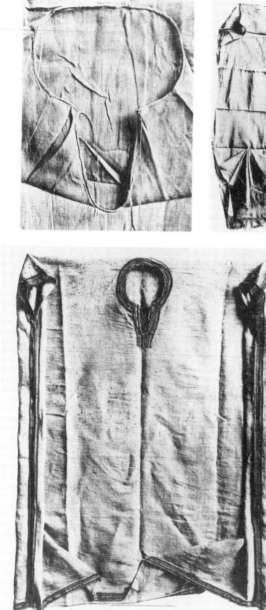

25. (Above) One of Kha's newly laundered sleeveless shirts, which displays tie-cords, a fringed hem and storage folds. (After Schiaparelli, *Relazione*, II, 1927, fig. 68.)

26. (Left) Kha's winter tunic with applied tapestry-woven bands. (After Schiaparelli, *Relazione*, II, 1927, fig. 69.)

and his wife Merit at Deir el-Medina (Theban Tomb 8) was discovered by Schiaparelli in 1906. The contents, including Kha's abundant and well preserved wardrobe, are now in the Museo Egizio, Turin. Although Schiaparelli's textile descriptions are woefully inadequate, much can fortunately be deduced from his excellent publication photographs.

Kha's wardrobe, stored in several chests and a sack, comprised approximately fifty trianglar loincloths and twenty-six shirts, seven of which were found with a triangular loincloth, each constituting a set. The loincloths were mostly newly laundered, the few dirty examples being kept separately. All the shirts have the same knee-length dimensions. Schiaparelli believed that Kha's garments had been pressed with a heavy implement before storage; certainly impressions of the tie-cords are sometimes clearly visible on the tunic fabric below. Seventeen sleeveless tunics, three bearing fringes, are all of 'thin' cloth, with the exception of a heavier ornamented winter tunic. Tapestry-woven

27. Merit's folded dressing gown *(right)* as found in the basket *(left)* with a possible wig curler *(below)*. (After Schiaparelli, *Relazione*, II, 1927, fig. 80.)

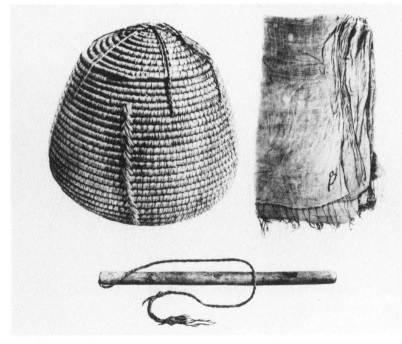

bands in warp-weave are applied to its sides and hemline, at both front and back, and around the neck. This finely preserved winter tunic was rolled up with two fringed 'tablecloths' (undoubtedly women's cloaks), in a fine sack displaying decorative fringes. Four shawls complete the inventory and, significantly, Schiaparelli remarks that they are of a type rarely depicted in reliefs.

Merit's dressing gown was found neatly folded in a basket also containing plaited hair, a comb and a possible wig curler. Presumably a prized garment, it consists of a wide fringed sheet, completely spotted with oil, and bearing Merit's own enigmatic ink laundry mark. An interesting parallel is a Sixth Dynasty dressing gown, excavated by Schiaparelli in 1920, from a tomb at Gebelein. Two additional side sections of fringed material have here been added to the open central front, to be wrapped right over the body.

Warm bedcovers with pile and folded sheets were found on Merit's bed. Similar bedclothes piled on a bed were discovered by Winlock in 1920 in the intact tomb of Wah, the estate manager of Meket-Re. Both Wah's kilt and several sheets had originally belonged to other people, one even to the King Mentuhotep II, as the laundry marks prove.

Household fabrics comprise Kha's cushioning, mats and two warp-weave tapestries, used either as furniture coverings or as

28. Merit's bed displaying warm bedcovers with pile and folded sheets. (After Schiaparelli, *Relazione*, II, 1927, fig. 105.)

29. The reverse of a warp-weave tapestry displaying looping, from the tomb of Kha. The obverse lotus flowers and buds design is clearly visible. (After Schiaparelli, *Relazione*, II, 1927, fig. 116.)

window hangings. Executed in coarse but close weave, extra warps are floating, as opposed to being knotted, over several wefts to form looping on the reverse. The obverse is thus divided into horizontal bands by the wefts. Two narrow coloured stripes at each end mark off a wide border, containing a graceful design of lotus flowers and buds. Single, wider stripes intrude into the field from the two selvedges to form open compartments, likewise containing lotus flowers and buds.

Even this cursory review of selected extant textiles has answered many questions posed by the monumental depictions, although sometimes simultaneously presenting irreconcilable divergences. It is to be hoped that new discoveries and research will provide even more solutions.

6
Tutankhamun's wardrobe

The textiles of Tutankhamun, together with four linens from the tomb of Tuthmosis IV and the 'girdle' of Ramesses III, provide a tantalising glimpse into the nature and extent of a Pharaoh's wardrobe during the New Kingdom. The position of Keeper of the Royal Wardrobe was, however, of long standing, being attested as early as the First Dynasty.

An inkling of the vastness of Tutankhamun's wardrobe is afforded both by Carter's often inadequate notes and by Burton's photographic record. The boy king's underwear alone comprised shirts, with beautifully hemmed necklines, and over a hundred triangular loincloths, sometimes found in sets with kilts. The remains of nearly fifty child's garments and shawls were discovered, together with belts, scarfs, caps and headdresses. One royal kerchief even proved useful to the ancient tomb robbers for knotting solid gold rings. Tutankhamun also possessed nearly thirty gloves, or archer's driving gauntlets, with tapes for tying at the wrist, a fingerstall and a sling bandage.

Linen was generally used for wrapping funerary equipment. The famous jackal shrine was covered by a child's shirt, shawl and scarf, all now in the Victoria and Albert Museum. The shirt bears the date of the seventh regnal year of Akhenaten, possibly the year of Tutankhamun's birth. Carter lists over a hundred 'bundles', 'rolls' and 'pads' of cloth, all of undetermined contents. These still remain unwrapped because of their extremely delicate condition, caused primarily by dampness, but also by their rough repacking in boxes following the tomb's plundering shortly after the king's death. Deterioration has likewise progressed since 1922; colours observed by Carter were either darkened or barely distinguishable when examined by Pfister just fifteen years later. Unfortunately only eighteen of the most spectacular Cairo linens have ever been scientifically published.

Some garments are decorated with astonishing diversity, using beads and metalwork. Applied rosettes and sequins were popular, one tunic displaying three thousand gold rosettes. Often these inlays are all that remains, as with the pall and king's beaded kilt, because Carter decided to sacrifice the decayed cloth in preference to its decorative elements. This kilt is striped in beadwork of varied colours and the Victoria and Albert Museum possesses a similar incomplete belt of beadwork and gilt

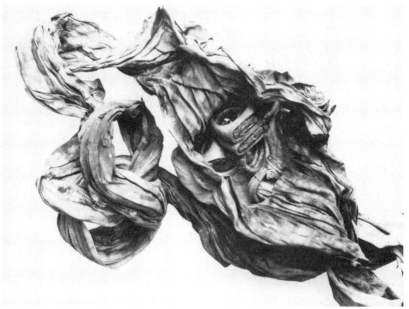

30. Tutankhamun's kerchief, used by the ancient tomb robbers for knotting solid gold rings. (Courtesy of the Griffith Institute, Oxford.)

bracteates. The remains of two sleeveless corselets utilise gold, carnelian, coloured inlay and faience. A more practical cuirass of leather scales was also found. A priestly leopardskin and two cloth imitations bear gilded wooden heads with solid gold claws and five-pointed stars.

Woven patterned bands, sewn in or inwoven, and embroidery are characteristic. The bands mostly appear down the sides and around the bottom of the skirt, above a fringed hem formed from warp-ends. Applied collars are frequent. A yellow tapestry-woven tunic, with green and dark brown narrow stripes, has bands of green flying ducks. Another bears rows of rosettes, an inscribed central band and perhaps wings, with a floral broad collar completing the ornamentation.

The celebrated dalmatic-like garment, commonly known as 'King Tutankhamun's tunic' (Cairo 642), merits particular attention. This sleeved robe of fine plain linen bears applied bands, both in pattern-weave and embroidery, and a fringed hem. It was made from a folded length of cloth. The side selvedges were sewn together leaving openings for sleeve insertion. A hole and vertical slit for the neck, decorated with an applied embroidered

31. The famous jackal shrine *(above)* covered by a child's shirt, shawl and scarf; the docket on the child's shirt *(left)* bears a seventh regnal year date of Akhenaten. (Courtesy of the Griffith Institute, Oxford.)

ankh-shaped chest piece, were cut in the front. As the garment would have reached to well below the knee, and the sleeves to at least the wrist of the boy king, it would have required a supporting belt. The indications are, however, that this state robe had never been worn.

The prevailing colour was originally blue, with supplementary red, green and dark brown hues. Now it is completely and irreparably black. The woven bands, forming side borders at both front and back, are of warp-face weave with weft concealed, creating a pattern of squares, checks, zigzags, chevrons and diamonds. The warp-weave collar, originally drawn in and tied with two tie-cords, carries juxtaposed cartouches around the centre, containing the Pharaoh's *prenomen,* bordered by geometric patterns.

The embroidered border, on front and back, and the bands forming the cross were worked separately as small squares and sewn together before application. The open-weave linen ground originally rendered the fine embroidery, in blue, green and white threads, clearly distinguishable. The compositions were arranged in small panels with the subjects alternately light on a dark background, and vice versa. The designs are distinctly Syrian in derivation, although displaying marked Egyptian influence. The winged female sphinxes and griffins with interspersed palmettes

32. Tutankhamun's sleeved tunic with applied pattern-woven and embroidered bands. (Courtesy of the Griffith Institute, Oxford.)

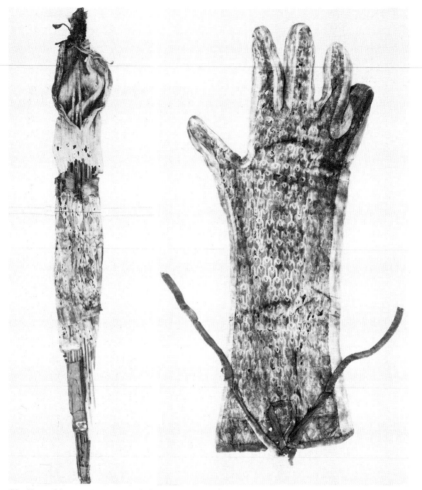

33. Tutankhamun's quiver *(left)* and one glove *(right)*, both displaying tapestry-woven motifs. (Courtesy of the Griffith Institute, Oxford.)

are typical Mesopotamian and Syrian motifs, but the cartouche and *djed*-pillar with their pendant uraeii form solely Egyptian elements. Likewise, the galloping, biting animals are of distinctly alien extraction, whereas the peaceful mingling of bulls, ibex and gazelle, juxtaposed with their terrified flight from the lions and trained dogs, is characteristically Egyptian.

Further decorated linens comprise a quiver, with a design of

34. Tapestry-woven fabric bearing the cartouche of Amenophis II, from the tomb of Tuthmosis IV. (Cairo JE 46526; after Carter and Newberry, *The Tomb of Thoutmôsis IV*, 1904, plate X.)

lotus flowers and buds, and a bag and gloves displaying feather patterning. A conscious adaptation of the latter motif, and one frequently appearing in pictorial representations of royal kilts, is a warp-weave textile, originally sewn on to a garment, bearing rows of paired chevrons.

Four fabrics from the tomb of Tuthmosis IV, also excavated by Carter in 1903, provide the earliest surviving examples of tapestry weaving using blue, red, yellow, green and dark brown threads. At least three were prized heirlooms, fragments of ceremonial garments, two perhaps over fifty years old, bearing the names of his grandfather, Tuthmosis III, and his father, Amenophis II. The latter cloth has both inscriptional and floral ornamentation, with crowned uraeii flanking the cartouche, and eight rows of alternating lotus flowers and papyrus inflorescence. Borders to the left and right respectively display alternate lotus flowers and buds, and a double row of alternating semicircles. Contrasting colours are similarly applied throughout. Dark brown (now black) whipping stitches divide these borders from the central design. A fourth fragment bears pink and green rosettes between narrow intersecting bands, both the products of weft insertion during weaving.

The famous so-called 'girdle' of Ramesses III, now in Liverpool, was probably a band forming part of a king's jacket. Bought at Thebes in 1855, it is a compound cloth measuring 17 feet (5.2 m) long, and tapering from 5 inches (127 mm) to 1⅞ inches (48

35. The 'girdle' of Ramesses III, section actual size. (After Lee, in *Liverpool Annals*, V, 1913, plate XI; now Merseyside County Museums M 11156.)

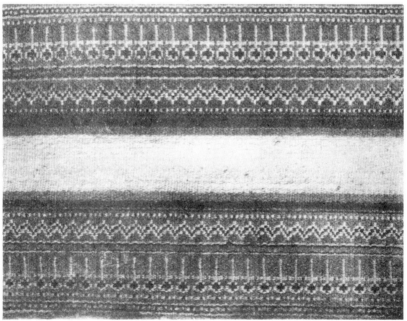

mm) in width. The design, formed by extra warp threads creating a pair of longitudinal stripes, is separated by a central plain linen band. Evidently commenced at the wide end, it was finished at the narrow end by gradually dropping the required number of warps.

The stripes are ornamented with zigzags, dots and rows of *ankh* signs, executed in very fine weave, using blue, red, yellow, green and white linen. The narrow end, on both faces, bears the sadly deteriorated black ink cartouches and second regnal year date of the monarch. Although woven on a simple loom, and probably taking from three to four months to complete, the textile is of excellent workmanship with surprisingly few weaving flaws considering its extreme complexity. A parallel to the 'girdle' is the braid from the saddlecloth, found upside down on the horse mummy, belonging to Hatshepsut's favourite Senenmut. Also a compound cloth, its geometrical pattern is formed of coloured warps.

Writing of Tutankhamun's wardrobe in 1923, Carter remarked that 'the material from this tomb will be of supreme importance to the history of textile art and it needs very careful study.' Regrettably, as many questions remain unanswered, as they did to Carter, and will now never be solved. The royal wardrobe door is indeed only slightly ajar!

7
The Egyptian laundry

The ancient Egyptians possessed more underwear than any other type of clothing, and they washed this much more frequently than they did their outer garments. Whilst the vast majority of the population would have relied on the women doing the household washing on the banks of the Nile, an age-old practice which still continues, the concern here is with the professional laundry, serving the households of the élite, and which was always a male concern.

Washermen are mentioned from the Old Kingdom onwards and were semi-independent people attached either to the households of the well-to-do, or else in the service of large temple institutions, such as Karnak and Medinet Habu, or of the king himself. The Superintendent of the Washermen seems to have ranked slightly lower than the Sandal Bearer as an intimate member of the Pharaoh's or provincial nomarch's personal entourage. He was also an important member of a rich household, and it seems that the office could sometimes be held by a son of the head of the house. Amongst other craftsmen the position was also reasonably important, judging by the fact that on the West Bank at Thebes in the Late New Kingdom there was one washerman to every thirty households. As most of these inhabitants would have been simple people who could not have afforded to use the professional service, some idea of its significance can be gauged. At the workmen's village at Deir el-Medina washermen even formed their own guild and were probably paid by the government.

Laundering activities are shown in a few isolated tomb reliefs, where a study of both the scenes and the appropriate hieroglyphic captions enables the various stages to be reconstructed. There are six unequivocal laundry scenes from the Middle Kingdom, four at Beni Hasan and one each at Deir el-Gebrawi and Aswan. From these it is evident that the dirty linen was first rolled up into a ball before being wetted. The 'soap' or natron (sodium carbonate and sodium bicarbonate) was then rubbed into the cloth. Natron was used for bleaching linen in Egypt into the nineteenth century. It would have been much needed in the New Kingdom to clean the diaphanous best garments of the rich, shown in banquet scenes in the tomb paintings to be stained on their upper parts. Doubtless this was caused by the melting of perfume cones adorning the

36. Modern laundry by Egyptian women at the riverbank. (Courtesy of Mr Martin Vincent.)

wigs, which would have dripped oil, resulting in the characteristic reddish yellow staining on clothing.

Wooden clubs seem to have been used for beating cloth still immersed in water, but generally it had been removed to a stone support. Alternatively stones were used as a beating mechanism. The laundry was then rinsed in running water before being shaken to get rid of excess moisture. For the wringing process an upright pole was placed in the ground and a piece of laundry was wound on to it. A stick, stuck through the other end of the cloth, was turned around to perform the wringing action on the now twisted fabric. The tomb scenes clearly show the water streaming out as a result of this action. Each item then had to be stretched with force to press out the last drops, generally by two men holding each end by its small sides and then leaning right back diametrically. The laundry was spread out to dry on the bleaching ground, after which larger items, such as sheets, were folded. The clean washing was packed in a large bundle, consisting of a separate piece of cloth knotted together at its ends, for transport. Generally the final scene shows the chief washerman carrying the bundle away on his head.

37. The Superintendent of the Washermen carrying a pleating board, below the Sandal Bearer, behind their master. From the tomb of Senbi at Meir, Twelfth Dynasty. (After Blackman, *Meir*, I, 1914, plate II.)

The one clear laundry scene of the New Kingdom shows that certain refinements have entered the craft. The tomb of Ipuy (Theban Tomb 217) at Deir el-Medina shows two men washing in two large lug-handled pottery tubs near a canal or the river. The left-hand tub stands in a hurdle, indicating that the water inside could be heated, perhaps using hot charcoal. The dirty laundry was doubtless soaked in the cold water in the other tub before being transferred to the warm water for the natron washing. To the left, two more men take the wet laundry from a tub and beat it on a stone. The register above shows pieces of cloth spread out for drying after having been rinsed in the river.

38. (Above) Laundry scene. From the tomb of Khnemhotep at Beni Hasan, Twelfth Dynasty. (After Newberry, *Beni Hasan*, I, 1893, plate XXIX.)

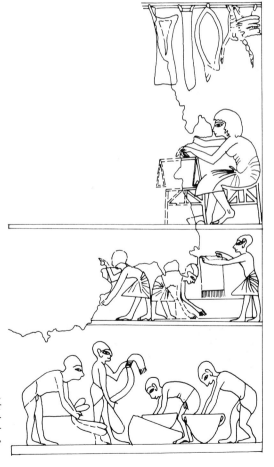

39. (Right) Laundry scene. From the tomb of Ipuy at Deir el-Medina, Nineteenth Dynasty. (After Davies, *Two Ramesside Tombs at Thebes*, 1927, plate XXVIII.)

Pleating was performed while the cloth was still damp. The garments would have been inside out, this being the most professional manner in which to wash and dry clothing. It was also the most natural way of removing a tight-fitting tunic with very narrow wrists. It is possible that the activity is depicted in the top register of the Ipuy scene, where a man sits on a stool and pleats garments before hanging them on a line to dry. As the relief is very fragmentary, it is impossible to know whether he is using the peculiar wooden instrument which is depicted at Meir being carried over the shoulder of the chief washerman. Three enigmatic objects, albeit bearing no relation to the Meir instrument, survive in the collections of the British Museum, Florence and Turin. They have been interpreted as pleating boards, with the cloth being pressed into the concave grooves of the upper surface of the hardwood. The ridges in the material could then have been fixed with a gelatinous sizing, which would at least explain the yellow tint sometimes employed by Egyptian artists in showing pleated clothing. It appears much more likely, however, that the Ipuy pleater is simply working by hand, pinching the wet fabric with his fingers. The folded material could then have been tightly bound with cords and allowed to dry. This method would additionally have required no sizing, and, although a time-consuming exercise, the labour supply was abundant in ancient Egypt.

40. An alleged wooden pleating board, views from above and the side. (BM 35908. Courtesy of the Trustees of the British Museum.)

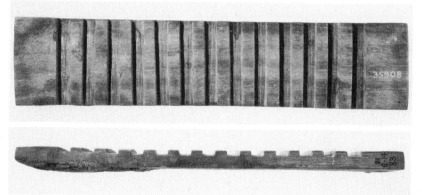

The newly laundered textiles were stored either in linen chests or, in poorer households, in pots. The chests were lockable, with a cord being wound around projecting knobs in the body of the box and the lid. Wet clay, embossed with the owner's mark, completed the seal. This demonstrates that linen was a precious household commodity, and it was from this store that garments were taken to clothe or accompany the deceased. This explains why inverted, newly laundered linens, often displaying regular folds as if taken from a box, are found in a funerary context.

Laundry marks are mainly illustrated on linens found in the Eleventh Dynasty tomb of the slain soldiers at Deir el-Bahri and from Kha's wardrobe. The former series used indelible ink, whilst on the latter both ink and embroidery are visible. The mass burial of the sixty slain Theban soldiers serving under Mentuhotep I, excavated by Winlock in 1926, contained a wealth of textiles now in the Metropolitan Museum, New York. Sixty marks were found in the corners or near the fringes of kilts, bed sheets and bath towels. All were written in black ink, except for five where red was used. Twenty-nine pieces bear a sign resembling a truncated obelisk projecting above another structure, with the sun disc above producing two rays of light on each side thus: 𝍩. The sign was probably used to denote linen from the Mentuhotep temple stores at Deir el-Bahri, carried by the soldiers as part of their expedition equipment to the north, where they perished. A

41. Three enigmatic ink laundry marks on sheets belonging to the slain soldiers, from their tomb at Deir el-Bahri, Eleventh Dynasty. (MMA 27.3.105; .107; .108. Courtesy of the Metropolitan Museum of Art, Rogers Fund, 1927.)

further twenty-six linens bear the names of the owners of the
sheets, sometimes with the name of the man's father and more
rarely that of his grandfather as well. In two cases the mother's
name appears. As no titles or indications of professions are given,
it seems that these are identifying laundry marks rather than
post-mortem labelling by embalmers. The remaining five marks
are all enigmatic signs, clearly serving to identify frequently
laundered sheets and garments. Kha's linens bear his name and
his particular marks, namely an ⋈ or, less frequently, a simple ✕
sign. Embroidered marks simply reflect the architect's higher
official status.

42. Laundry list. Pottery ostracon (actual size), of the first regnal year of Seti I, listing in
hieratic the delivery to the riverbank of ten kilts, eight loincloths and five sanitary towels,
from Deir el-Medina, Nineteenth Dynasty. (After Černý's facsimile, ODeM 30.)

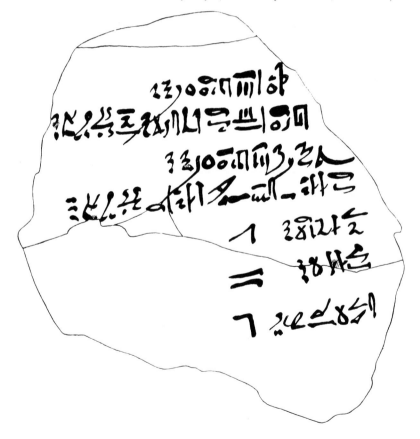

Complete laundry lists survive from Deir el-Medina written in the cursive hieratic script on broken pottery sherds, or more rarely limestone flakes, known as ostraca. Those with high totals represent the lists of the washermen, perhaps deliveries to the gang, whilst others with low numbers are the amounts of dirty washing from individual households in the village.

The haphazard arrangement of some lists suggests hasty scribbling, perhaps by the housewife herself, but generally a fixed order of items is shown. This corresponds to the most frequently washed garments, with the kilt, worn by both sexes and the most common garment in the village, at the head of the list. It is followed by the triangular loincloth worn by both sexes, women's pants (?), and then sleeves for adults and children. The cloak, mainly worn by women, does not occur frequently, but when it does it jumps to the head of the list as the most important garment. Other items of dress are those worn by both sexes such as tunics, kerchiefs used to protect the head, especially when winnowing, and sashes worn both around the waist and crosswise around the upper part of the body. A special type of woman's shawl is also mentioned, clearly differing from the normal cloak. Smaller items are handkerchieves, bands, rags and even sanitary towels. The last, which have the literal translation from the Egyptian of 'bands of the behinds', were specifically made from a piece of worn fabric. Sheets and bath towels appear as important laundered household linens. Even the quality of individual items can be recorded, using descriptive terms such as 'smooth cloth', 'in a good state' and 'threadbare'.

Sometimes the dirty washing even had to be delivered to the riverbank, indicating that the laundrymen were not necessarily responsible for its collection. Nevertheless, this did not prevent one washerman in the village from complaining that he had too much washing from too many houses, and also that insufficient soap was supplied to him. He demanded a reduction in the number of houses he served from eight to four per day and complained that the Pharaoh had originally allocated him only three houses daily.

There are references to the work of the laundry in the surviving literature. The New Kingdom copy of the composition *The Satire on the Trades* contains a passage bemoaning the drawbacks of the washerman's task: 'The washerman washes on the riverbank being near to the crocodile. "Father, I go away from the flowing water," says his son or his daughter, "to a job that satisfies me more than all [other] jobs." His foot is soiled by dirt, no limb of his is clean. He sets to work on the garment of a woman who has her period. He spends the day with the beating-stick and a stone. One says to him: "Dirty linen! Come to me! The basket overflows with it." ' However, the reverse aspect is portrayed in a passage from a contemporary love song: 'Would I were the laundryman of my sister (beloved) for a single month. I would enjoy my [work of washing the garment] that had touched her body. I would be the man who washed out the ointment which is in her kerchief. I would work myself to the bone on her frocks!'

This composite picture of the Egyptian laundry, derived from various sources, gives the general impression of the extreme cleanliness of the ancient Egyptians.

8
Sewing and darning

As the Egyptians were inclined to use the verb 'to make' for the dressmaking process, while a specific word 'to sew' was used for making stitches, the latter occurs much less frequently. The term for sewing was used synonymously to cover the darning of textiles, as a specific word for mending related only to basketry and wooden objects. High standards were attained in both areas and all the requisite equipment was possessed from the earliest times.

Metal scissors and knives were used for the initial cutting of the woven cloth. Needles or bodkins, made of wood, bone, copper/ bronze or even gold and silver, survive in large numbers. Although they tend to be larger and coarser than their modern counterparts and display marked domed heads, many possess minute eyes for extremely fine sewing. They often survive threaded with their original flax, coloured for embroidery, and one example, from Amarna, bears two eyes placed at right angles, enabling two threads to be sewn at the same time. Metal pins are also larger, at about 2 inches (50 mm), than their modern equivalents and tend to possess loop heads. They thus probably served a dual function and could be left in the hole as a decorative fastening mechanism for the completed garment. Even thorns have been found acting as substitutes for metal pins. Needle cases for storage utilise the hollow bone of a bird or simply comprise a piece of reed bound round with cloth.

The balls of flax thread are usually found wound on to a flax waste core. Reels or bobbins of wood, limestone, pottery or faience survive in quite large numbers. There is one known example of a Dynastic thimble, which is now in the Metropolitan Museum. Excavated at the Late New Kingdom village at Lisht, this sandstone object is concave at one side and grooved on the other. It seems to have been worn over the middle finger and was held in place by the index and third fingers. Long wear had turned a small circular socket, provided near one end of the groove for the head of the needle, into a hole running right through the thimble.

A study of dressmaking techniques on garments reveals that both seams and hems were generally rolled and the fabric was then secured by whipping stitches, which are often crude and pass from back to front. However, other seams were mainly of the flat ('tatbeet') type, and the very similar run and fell seam, which is particularly suited for clothes subject to frequent wear and washing, was used for children's sleeves. The only difference between the two types is that the flat seam has not been cut down during construction. Both the antique seam, for joining narrow selvedges, and the faggoted seam, used for decoration, are found on early dresses, although they would have been obscured by the ornamental extended weft fringes. Sometimes a few inches were left unsewn at the bottom seams of a garment to give greater freedom in walking. Buttonholed hems in blanket stitch were a Coptic innovation.

Embroidered textiles comprising thread sewn on in a design are rare and not typical of Egyptian workmanship. Many reported examples, often based on the opinions of the initial excavators, who were not textile experts, can on re-examination be relegated to the category of weaving techniques. Applied needlework was not popular and even in the Coptic Period stitches were rarely used for their own sake. Rather, the aim was to fill in an area by using a simple satin stitch, or to eke out a design hard to complete in weaving alone by laying down a few threads.

The major exceptions to this lack of embroidery are three of the tunics from Tutankhamun's tomb. The most splendid is the heavily ornamented dalmatic-like garment which has a wide band of squares across the bottom, each one containing an embroidered scene or motif. As most of these appear to be distinctly Syrian in character, one must speculate that they were executed by foreign craftsmen based, however, in the Pharaonic workshops and also using basic Egyptian motifs, such as the cartouche and uraeus. Both these tunics and the so-called 'embroideries' from the tomb of Tuthmosis IV have afforded an insight into known needlework stitches. Coloured linen threads, in blue, pink, green and dark brown, were used to create running, straight, chain, arrowhead, satin and stem stitch. Both cross and stem stitch were employed for decorative couching on tunics in general. Laundry marks on the Kha linen were worked in coral and overcast stitch (over a running stitch base). These hand-sewn marks should not be confused with weavers' marks of identification deliberately woven into the fabric and not intended as decoration. However, as black ink laundry marks are the norm, the inference again is that embroidery was not popular and that ink was felt to be a much more satisfactory medium.

Funerary textiles, both garments and mummy wrappings, show extensive wear with frequent repairs. They were clearly adapted

43. (Left) Copper pin with loop head *(left);* silver needle *(centre);* copper needle *(right),* from Naqada, Predynastic. (UC 4301; 36151; 36154.)

44. (Centre) Bird's bone needle case containing fifteen bronze needles, unprovenanced, New Kingdom. (UC 7721.)

45. (Right) Sandstone thimble (actual size) from Lisht, Twentieth Dynasty. (MMA 11.151.634. Courtesy of the Metropolitan Museum of Art, Rogers Fund, 1911.)

from worn-out household linens, such as clothing, shawls and sheets. Mummy bandages, for example, were torn from old wide fabrics and not specifically woven as narrow tapes. They thus provide much information on the mending and darning techniques in vogue.

Darning in ancient Egypt resembled a modified couching, with supplementary warps being laid before wefts and the weft picks, that is the individual weft threads, being subsequently stitched. Four techniques are visible, all of which must have been produced using a needle. On solid fabric a close whipping over the laid weft appears; and on open fabric a turned chain stitch or a cross stitch was used, or else only the warp was laid, with the weft picks being sewn in back stitch. Patching was performed extremely rarely in the Dynastic Period but is attested by a neatly patched sheet discovered in Tomb 148b at Deshasheh. By the Coptic Period it had become a much more common technique than darning.

The time and effort devoted to such repairs demonstrates that linens were often prized heirlooms, as, for example, with mended garments in the tomb of Tuthmosis IV which display tapestry weaving bearing the cartouche of his father, Amenophis II, their original owner. The labour expended likewise reflects the monetary value of the textiles. Linen could form one of the main objects of the ancient tomb robbers, especially in the Old Kingdom, when new garments were sometimes especially woven for funerary use. At Deshasheh it was often found by Petrie to have been partially dragged out of the coffins. Doubtless such robberies helped encourage the substitution of wall reliefs for the actual material at subsequent periods, although in the course of the Great Tomb Robberies of the late Twentieth Dynasty much linen was stolen. Even the spectacular garments of Kha are mainly worn out; whipping stitches, for example, carefully hemmed a partly frayed edge on one of the architect's triangular shawls. Likewise bath towels from the tomb of the slain soldiers at Deir el-Bahri show similar mending by the simple whipping of the raw edges of the material after the frayed warp ends have been trimmed. However, such care was not systematically displayed for none of the cloth from the workmen's village at Amarna shows any signs of mending. Obviously textiles, as with pottery, were too readily available at the site to merit attention once damage had occurred.

46. Detail of darning, with close whipping over the laid weft, on a tunic from Tarkhan, Twenty-third Dynasty(?). (UC 28616Ci.)

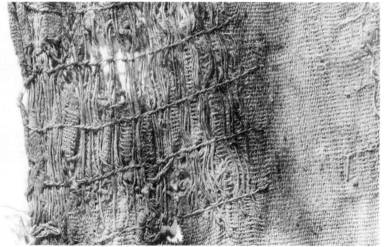

As complete sets of sewing artefacts are known from male burials, and as both the pictorial and textual evidence indicates men engaged in sewing garments, there is clear evidence that the craft was not exclusively a female pursuit. However, sewing and darning are likely to have been mainly the preserve of the female members of the Egyptian household and conducted on a non-profit-making basis. The presence of professional tailoring, as noted earlier, is impossible to gauge, but that life in general does not change is illustrated by a surviving letter addressed by a woman to her 'sister'. She requested a shawl to be woven 'before Amenophis comes', and a sanitary towel to be sewn for her, as she has 'nothing at all to wear'.

9
Dress and rank in ancient Egypt

A study of the commodity prices from the workmen's village at Deir el-Medina reveals the relative status of garments both in the household and on the trading market. The workmen possessed a few clothes of standard design, some of which were provided on the Pharaoh's account. Each man received one garment of a varying type, but always made of 'fine thin cloth'. However, as weaving and sewing still took place in the village, this distribution was clearly insufficient. Clothing was also valuable enough to be sometimes stolen.

An idea of the number of garments in a house is afforded by an unpublished ostracon with an object inventory. Furniture, bronze vessels, tools, basketry and wooden containers all occur in very low numbers, and mostly singly. The dress numbers, by contrast, are much higher. The list distinguishes three cloaks (used to create a draped woman's garment), ten kilts, of which six are 'in rags', that is worn out, and fifteen loincloths, of which nine are worn out. Two pairs of women's pants(?), one tunic, one sash, one pair of sleeves and two sheets are listed. The ostracon further records the presence of four pairs of sandals and eleven clews of yarn in this household.

The many ostraca listing prices reveal the tunic as the most commonly mentioned textile. It occurs in all four cloth qualities, although usually in the simplest category. As a standard product with a fixed price of five *deben*, about 450 grams (1 pound) of copper, it occurs very frequently in barter transactions. Surprisingly a sash could command exactly the same price, suggesting that our conceptions of value are much at variance with those of the ancient Egyptians.

The kilt, usually of 'thin cloth' but occurring in both the 'fine' and 'smooth' categories, could retail at up to twenty-five *deben*. The cloak, invariably of ordinary cloth, could also command the same price, presumably because of its extra fabric. Shawls and kerchiefs traded for as much as fifteen *deben*. Underwear was always cheaper than outer garments, although showing considerable price fluctuations. It was usually, for obvious reasons, of the 'thin cloth' quality, which was softer.

Sheets, normally of ordinary cloth, fetched double the price of a tunic, indicating that they were also approximately twice the size. One exceptionally high price for a sheet suggests a woollen blanket. Clearly cloth quality, its length and the condition of the textile were responsible for fixing the trading price on the exchange market. These first two factors also determined the initial price paid to the weaver.

In ancient Egypt the higher the rank of the citizen the more elaborate his garment became, and the more expensive its material. The vizier, the highest official, wore a particular dress consisting of a long straight skirt fitting tightly just above or below the breastline, and terminating at the ankles. It was held up by a narrow cord passing round the neck. The closer the individual to the royal court or capital, the more fashionable would be his tunic with triangular apron, both being elaborately pleated and using the finest gauze. Provincial styles are always somewhat outmoded. Conversely, the lower the citizen's status,

47. The dress of the vizier at Thebes, Eighteenth Dynasty. (After Davies, *The Tomb of the Vizier Ramose*, 1941, plates VI and XXXIX.)

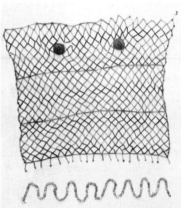

48. (Left) The 'dress' of a prostitute on the Turin 'Erotic' Papyrus 55001, Ramesside Period. (After Omlin, *Der Papyrus 55001*, 1973, plate XIII.)
49. (Above) Dancer's bead-net dress from tomb 978 at Qau, Fifth Dynasty. (UC 17743.)

the simpler and more scanty the mode of dress, and the cheaper the fabric. New Kingdom officers usually wore a tunic over a kilt, whereas the common soldiers were clad only in a kilt. Labourers wore a kilt, well suited to manual work, made of coarse, but subsequently warmer cloth. For the cold evenings a tunic was essential.

Art and sculpture aimed to render the form of the female body below a diaphanous garment. Children, however, ran around naked until reaching puberty. Nudity was in evidence amongst the lowest classes of Egyptian society, with serving girls and musicians being clad simply in a bead or shell girdle around the hips, and acrobatic dancers wearing a short patterned kilt. More decoration was applied directly to their bodies in the form of tattooed geometric designs. Prostitutes often displayed an image of the protective dwarf god Bes tattooed on to the upper thighs, doubtless serving as a seductive charm.

Bead-net dresses are seen on relief and statuary placed over the dress already being worn by respectable ladies, to create the effect of a patterned fabric with the use of many semi-precious materials. However, worn alone by dancers and prostitutes, such dresses were clearly designed to be sexually evocative. The Petrie Museum possesses a rare example of such a bead-net dress, found

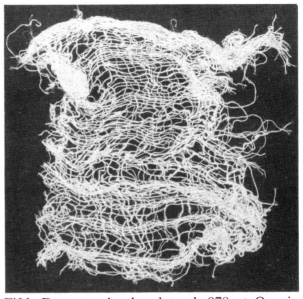

50. 'Fishing-net' linen from tomb 99 at Deshasheh, Fifth Dynasty. (UC 31209.)

in a box in the Fifth Dynasty plundered tomb 978 at Qau in Middle Egypt. Partial rethreading has created a wide-meshed network of blue and black faience cylinder beads with green faience ring beads placed in between. A string of *Mitra* shells at the bottom would have rattled when the wearer danced. Two small caps were provided for wearing over the breasts, made of blue faience with the nipples in black faience. Four small holes were pierced around the base for threading into the appropriate position on the network.

The 'fishing-net' dress would have had a similar appeal in a boating situation. It is so named after a famous passage in Papyrus Westcar of the Old Kingdom which describes girls from King Snefru's harem clad in such garments in order to row the Pharaoh on his lake and thus amuse him out of his ennui. Such a dress was much more likely to have been of linen than of beads, especially if it was the sole garment to be worn, as it would have been rendered even more transparent and clinging when wet. A very openly woven linen fragment, of only thirty by twenty threads to the inch, in the Petrie Museum, is possibly from such a garment. Petrie, who discovered it in the Fifth Dynasty tomb 99 at Deshasheh, detached this sample from a larger piece of fabric of unspecified size and immediately drew the analogy with Papyrus Westcar.

51. Professional women's mourning dress, Eighteenth Dynasty. (After Davies, *The Tomb of Nefer-Hotep at Thebes*, I, 1933, plate XXII.)

Another specific type of woman's garment was mourning dress. Wailing women, the professional mourners at a New Kingdom funeral, appear bare-breasted. The normal draped garment was taken off the shoulders and was knotted, or else tied with a sash, just below the bustline. Grey streaks on the dress were the result of the dust thrown on to the head. Book of the Dead vignettes often show their female owners depicted in the same fashion.

From the few examples cited above, it is evident that dress could function as a status symbol in ancient Egypt. Its role can be evaluated both by a study of textile prices and by viewing specific types of garments worn by various elements in her society.

52. (Opposite) Map of ancient Egypt, showing the sites mentioned in the text. (Drawn by D. R. Darton.)

10
Museums to visit

Egyptian textiles have mostly been individually published in scientific journals. There is no general book on the subject, apart from this one. The reader must therefore view the evidence for himself by visiting some of the following museum collections which have Egyptian textiles on exhibition or contain items specifically mentioned in the text. Although this book has been concerned with Dynastic textiles, some collections primarily of Coptic textiles are included in the list; these are denoted by an asterisk.

United Kingdom
Bolton Museum and Art Gallery*, Le Mans Crescent, Bolton, Lancashire BL1 1SA. Telephone: Bolton (0204) 22311 extension 379.
British Museum, Great Russell Street, London WC1B 3DG. Telephone: 01-636 1555 or 1558.
City of Bristol Museum and Art Gallery, Queens Road, Bristol BS8 1RL. Telephone: Bristol (0272) 299771.
Manchester Museum, University of Manchester, Oxford Road, Manchester M13 9PL. Telephone: 061-273 3333.
Merseyside County Museums*, William Brown Street, Liverpool L3 8EN. Telephone: 051-207 0001 or 5451.
Petrie Museum of Egyptian Archaeology, University College London, Gower Street, London WC1E 6BT. Telephone: 01-387 7050 extension 617.
Victoria and Albert Museum*, Cromwell Road, South Kensington, London SW7 2RL. Telephone: 01-589 6371.
Whitworth Art Gallery*, University of Manchester, Whitworth Park, Manchester M15 6ER. Telephone: 061-273 4865.

Belgium
Musées Royaux d'Art et d'Histoire, Parc de Cinquantenaire, 10 Brussels.

Canada
Royal Ontario Museum, 100 Queen's Park, Toronto, Ontario.

Egypt
Egyptian Antiquities Museum, Tahrir Square, Cairo.

France
Musée du Louvre, Palais du Louvre, 75003, Paris.

Italy
Museo Archeologico, Via Colonna 96, Florence.
Museo Egizio, Palazzo dell' Accademia delle Scienze, Via Accademia delle Scienze 6, Turin.

Netherlands
*Gemeentemuseum**, Prinsessegracht 30, 2514 AP, The Hague, Zuid Holland.

United States of America
*Brooklyn Museum**, 200 Eastern Parkway, Brooklyn, New York 11238.
Metropolitan Museum of Art, 5th Avenue at 82nd Street, New York, NY 10028.
Museum of Fine Arts, Huntington Avenue, Boston, Massachusetts 02115.
*Textile Museum**, 2320 South Street NW, Washington, DC 20008.
University Museum, University of Pennsylvania, 33rd and Spruce Streets, Philadelphia, Pennsylvania 19104.

Acknowledgements

I owe an incalculable debt to the many textile experts who have continually assisted and encouraged my researches. Mrs Joan Allgrove McDowell, Professor Elizabeth Barber, Miss Elisabeth Crowfoot, Mrs Karen Finch, Mr Donald King, Mrs Sheila Landi, Mrs Lidia Pedrini and Miss Nora Scott represent just a few of the many professionals with whom I have had contact.

I wish to express my thanks to the various museums which have allowed me to view their Dynastic textiles, and which have provided photographs and permission for publication. In particular, Dr Peter Lacovara of the Egyptian Department, Museum of Fine Arts, Boston, has engaged in considerable correspondence with me regarding the 'Boston dresses'. Mr Peter Harrison, Head of the Central Photographic Unit, University College London, deserves high praise for his ever sensitive approach to the photographing of Egyptian antiquities, many examples of which appear here for the first time. All are the copyright of the Department of Egyptology, University College London. The line drawings are the work of Dr Stuart Munro-Hay.

Professor J. J. Janssen generously spent his time in translating the unpublished laundry lists and provided his usual immense moral support and encouragement. Acknowledgement is made to Dr W. J. Murnane and Penguin Books Ltd for permission to reproduce the Chronology. Mrs Barbara Adams, Editor of the Shire Egyptology series, has willingly answered my numerous queries throughout the writing of this book.

Index

Page numbers in italic refer to illustrations